Devotions from a Jou

A Closer Walk with God
Devotions from a Journey Through the Holy Lands

Sue Loeffler

A Closer Walk with God

Proisle Publishing Services LLC
1177 6th Ave 5th Floor
New York, NY 10036, USA
Phone: (+1 347-922-3779)

PROISLE PUBLISHING
SERVICES LLC
info@proislepublishing.com

A CLOSER WALK WITH GOD
Copyright © 2022 by Sue Loeffler

All rights reserved by the author. No part of this book may be reproduced or transmitted in any form or by any means, electronic or mechanical, including photocopying, recording, or by any information storage and retrieval system, without permission in writing from the copyright owner.

The views expressed in this work are solely those of the author and do not necessarily reflect the views of the publisher, and the publisher disclaims any responsibility for them.

References used:

He Walked with Us by Merilyn Copland, PhD
Answereth a Matter website by Steve Siefker
Holy Bible NIV and ESV
Personal notes on my journey through the Holy Lands

Printed in the United States of America

ISBN: 979-8-9860972-0-6

Devotions from a Journey Through the Holy Lands

Draw near to God and He will draw near to you.

James 4:8

A Closer Walk with God

A Closer Walk with God

Devotions from a Journey Through the Holy Lands

Sue Loeffler

Devotions from a Journey Through the Holy Lands

A Closer Walk with God

Introduction viii
Spring of Living Water 1
Mountain of Choices 5
Zeal for God 9
How do the Mighty Fall? 11
God Wins 15
Extravagant Love 17
The Lord is With You 19
Mighty God 21
The Chief Cornerstone 25
The Gates of Hell 33
Try Again 31
God's Judgement 33
Mountain of Majesty 35
Jesus' Hometown 37
Quiet! Be Still! 41
Jesus' Greatest Sermon 43
A Boy's Offering 47
Village by the Sea 59
Obedience Matters to God 53
God's Meeting Place 57
Herod's Beachfront Property 61
A Time of Blessing 63
A Mighty Fortress 65

Love Your Enemies	67
A Time of Testing	69
Don't Forget	71
The Way of the Cross	73
The Good News was Preached	77
Trust God First	79
The Agony and the Ecstasy	83
The Healing Pool	87
Bread of Life	89
God Has No Limits	91
Five Stones	93
Don't Worry	95
Writing on the Wall	97
No Complaints	99
Moab Hospitality	102
People of God	105
The Lost City	107
The Judgement Seat	109

Devotions from a Journey Through the Holy Lands

Introduction

Gaza was one of the five major Philistine cities in the Bible. Our tour did not take us there because of continuing problems on the Gaza Strip. The name *Gaza* means "strong" or "stronghold," but the city has been conquered so many times it has taken on the negative meaning of *Hell*. Think of the impact that gives to the story of the Ethiopian eunuch who had been to Jerusalem to worship God. He was on his way to Gaza when he stopped his chariot to read in the book of Isaiah.

God sent Philip to him at just the right time. "Do you understand what you are reading?" he asked.

"How can I unless someone explains it to me?" the Ethiopian said (Acts 8:31). He invited Philip to sit with him. The Ethiopian was reading: "He was led like a sheep to the slaughter, and as a lamb before the shearer is silent, so he did not open his mouth. In his humiliation, he was deprived of justice. Who can speak of his descendants? For his life was taken from the earth" (Isaiah 53:7-8).

Philip explained the good news of Jesus through this Scripture—that He suffered crucifixion for the forgiveness of our sins and rose from the dead for our eternal life. The two came to some water and Philip baptized the Ethiopian. Then Philip was taken away and the Ethiopian did not see him again.

Like this man on his way to Gaza, we are all destined for hell unless we come to know the saving grace of Jesus Christ. Nothing we do could ever make us worthy of God's salvation. Jesus did it all for us on the cross.

My purpose in writing this devotional book is to share how I was drawn closer to God as I hiked through ruins of old cities and walked the streets of modern cities of Israel and Jordan. The Bible stories came alive when I saw the countryside and the cities. It is my hope that you will be drawn closer to God too.

Prayer: *Lord God, make us more like Philip. Empower us with an urgency to tell people the good news that will save them from their sin and give them everlasting life. In Christ Jesus, Amen.*

Devotions from a Journey Through the Holy Lands

Spring of Living Water

En Gedi, an oasis in the Judean desert

The sound of children's laughter drew me up a rocky path to En Gedi, an oasis in the mountain desert near the Dead Sea. Men, women and children splashed in the waterfalls and pools. The spray from a waterfall cooled me from the intense heat. Healing water, rich with minerals, rose from springs deep within the earth. This is the water, which is often referred to in the Bible as living water. Moving, exhilarating water restored my soul.

Jesus talked about living water with the woman at the well (John 4). He was tired and thirsty from a long journey. The woman trudged to the well in the heat of the day. Jesus asked her for water and told her about water that would spring up into eternal life. He described worship that is in spirit and in truth, not tradition. Even though Jesus knew all about the woman's sinful life, He showed love and respect to her instead of judgment or rejection. Moved by his compassion, she left her water jug at the well and ran into Sychar to tell the people about a man who knew all about her. "Could this be the Christ?" she asked. Compelled by her story, the people walked out to meet Jesus and listened to what He had to say. They confessed to the woman, "Now we believe, not because of what you said: for we have heard him ourselves, and know that this is indeed the Christ, the Savior of the world" (John 4:42). They invited Jesus to stay with them a couple days, and because He did, more people believed.

Jesus knows what it feels like to grow tired and weary. He is aware of times we need rest and refreshment and often surprises us with an oasis of physical, emotional or spiritual renewal, which En Gedi was for me. I wanted to stay there, but Jesus led me home to tell people about the living water I found in Him when I visited Israel.

David found refuge at En Gedi when he was running for his life from King Saul but left the refreshing springs to become king. Ravens fed Elijah and he drank from the brook at the Kerith Ravine. As much as he probably wanted to linger there, God called him to defeat 450 prophets of Baal. The woman left the well, and while she was gone, Jesus said to the disciples, "I sent you to reap what you did not plant. Other men labored, and you have entered into their work (John 4:38). Even though the woman didn't hear Jesus' words, she demonstrated their meaning. She didn't go to Bible school or learn special techniques or big words. Empowered by the love Jesus showed her, she couldn't wait to tell others about Him.

Jesus met the woman's deepest need, the need to know Him. He also meets us at our point of need. He said, "Let anyone who is thirsty come to me and drink. Whoever believes in me, as the scripture has said, rivers of living water will flow from within them" (John 7:37-38). David responded to the love God showed him at En Gedi: "O God, you are my God: early will I seek you: my soul thirsts for you, my flesh longs for you as in a dry and weary land, where there is no water" (Psalm 63:1). The sons of Korah sang, "As the deer pants after the water brooks, so pants my soul for you, O God. My soul thirsts for God, for the living God (Psalm 42:1-2).

Jesus is our *Living Water*. He has promised us a future oasis in the New Jerusalem found in Revelation 22:1-7. The river of the water of life, as bright as crystal, will flow from the throne of God and run through the city. It will nourish the tree of life, which will bear a different fruit for every month of the year. Its leaves will heal the nations.

Prayer: *O Lord, draw us to the Spring of Living Water. Empower us to bring others to the life-changing water so they will experience hope instead of fear and peace instead of anxiety. In Christ Jesus, Amen.*

A Closer Walk with God

Devotions from a Journey Through the Holy Lands

Mountain of Choices

Statue of Elijah on the top of Mt. Carmel

The top of Mount Carmel in Israel bears a statue of Elijah. I gazed up at it and thought about what Elijah experienced—how he might have longed to stay at the Kerith Ravine where God sent ravens to feed him, and where he drank from the brook. However blessed Elijah felt, God intended the food and drink for the nourishment he needed to defeat 450 prophets of Baal. Led by King Ahab, the Israelites made the mistake of taking matters into their own hands instead of trusting God.

Desperate from a three-year drought, they did what the nations around them did when no harvests provided the food they needed. They prayed to Baal, the god of storms and fertility, to get them out of the mess they were in. They abandoned their faith in God and trusted Baal for rain and crops.

The biggest showdown in the Bible happened at Mount Carmel (1 Kings 18 ESV). The prophets set up their sacrifice and called to Baal from morning until night, for lightning to light the fire. The day grew long. Nothing happened. Elijah taunted Israel. "Maybe Baal was deaf, busy, taking a nap, or maybe he was on a trip. Maybe he was going to the bathroom!" The prophets shouted louder. They cut themselves so the mountain flowed with their blood. This was hard for me to imagine as I stood on top of Mount Carmel.

At the time of the evening sacrifice, it was Elijah's turn. He repaired the broken-down altar of God, laid his sacrifice on the wood, and had the people pour precious water on it and fill the surrounding trenches. Tension mounted as Elijah stepped forward and called out to God. "Let it be known today that you are God in Israel, and I am your servant and have done all these things at your command" (1 Kings 18:36 NIV).

Fire reached down and consumed the sacrifice, wood and stones. It licked up the water and burned the dirt. The people witnessed all this and fell on their faces crying, "The Lord—he is God! The Lord—he is God!"

This showdown reminded me of times I have taken matters into my own hands—times I rejected God's counsel, times which led to destruction and despair. Yet, God forgave me of my selfish, self-centered choices. He was faithful even when I was not. Like the Israelites, I was humbled and returned to God, my Savior.

Prayer: *O God, thank you for not giving up on us. You are compassionate and loving. Your mercies are new every morning. Search our hearts. Show us our idolatry and lack of faith in you. Light a fire in us so others will know you are God. Whatever situation we are in, help us to trust only You and nothing else—not our health, wealth, power or relationships. In Jesus' name, Amen.*

A Closer Walk with God

Zeal for God

The ruins of Megiddo today are in the midst of date palms, not present during the city's prosperity, but grew from seeds the excavation workers left from eating dates on the site.

The city of Megiddo was built high on a mountain over springs. Today a spiral staircase descends deep down to the water. Ruins of stone buildings stand as reminders of an ancient law in Israel that all buildings must be built with limestone, a law abided by in the twenty-first century. The cornerstone of each building aligns the stones vertically and horizontally, an image of Jesus as our cornerstone in relationships—first with God and then others.

Megiddo was located on a main international highway, which dominated trade routes from Egypt to Mesopotamia. Today, as in the past, Megiddo overlooks the fertile Jezreel Valley, the future site of Armageddon.

During the temple repair under King Josiah's reign, Hilkiah the high priest found the Book of the Law. Shaphan, the secretary, read the Law to the king. Josiah tore his robes and repented of the sins of his fathers. He renewed the covenant with God and removed all traces of Baal and Asherah worship. He did away with the pagan priests and demolished the dwellings of the male prostitutes in the temple. He got rid of the mediums and spiritists, the household gods, idols and all the other detestable things seen in Judah and Jerusalem (2 Kings 23:24).

After King Josiah re-established the temple, he met Neco, king of Egypt, at Carchemish on the Euphrates. Neco sent messengers to King Josiah saying, "What quarrel is there between you and me, O king of Judah? It is not you I am attacking at this time, but the house with which I am at war. God has told me to hurry: so stop opposing God, who is with me, or he will destroy you" (2 Chronicles 35:21).

Unfortunately, Josiah did not listen. He took on a fight that was not his and was killed. His rash conduct was the result of sincere but misguided zeal. Over confidence has destroyed many men throughout history. They could have avoided destruction if they had only trusted God.

Like Josiah, I've made wrong choices but did not die for them. This Scripture made me think how important it is to pay attention to what's happening and do what's right.

Thank you, Father God, for pursuing us, even when we fail, like Josiah, to listen to you. Open our eyes and hearts to do your will. In Christ Jesus, Amen.

How Do the Mighty Fall?

King Saul and his sons' bodies hung on the wall at Beth Shean for all to see.

I stood among the ruins of what was once a beautiful Philistine city. Beth Shean was located at the crossroads of the Jordan Valley and the Herod Valley.

Limestone streets lined with marble columns, Roman baths, temples, theaters and a market place told a story about a large metropolis, the capitol city of the Decapolis. One theater seated 7,000 people to enjoy Roman and Greek plays. Artistic mosaic floors greeted those who entered the huge baths. Heat rose from the stoves below to warm the stone floors.

During the time Beth Shean was a booming city, Israel wanted a king like Abimelech who reigned over the Philistines. Every nation had a king, and God gave Israel Saul. At first he did what was right, but later his pride got the best of him. He slipped away from God's commands. When he and his three sons, Jonathan, Abinadab and Malki-Shua, were killed in a battle on Mount Gilboa south of the city, their headless bodies were hung on the city walls of Beth Shean. Messengers carried their heads to every major Philistine city to show as their victory trophies (1 Chronicles 10:10 and 1 Samuel 31:10). Israelites from Jabesh Gilead came by night and took down the bodies of the king and his sons to give them a decent burial.

David lamented over the deaths of Saul and his sons: "Your glory, O Israel, lies slain on your heights. How the mighty have fallen!" (2 Samuel 1:19).

How did the mighty fall? Samuel, the prophet, had instructed Saul to destroy the Amalekites—all men, women, children and livestock, an extremely brutal command. Saul spared King Agag and the best of the sheep and cattle, fat calves and lambs—everything he thought was good. Then he went to Carmel and set up monuments in his own honor. Although Saul considered his incomplete obedience good enough, it grieved God. He was sorry He had made Saul king and judged his action as a complete rejection of His authority. Samuel's words had a devastating impact on the king: "To obey is better than sacrifice, and to heed is better than the fat of rams. For rebellion is like the sin of divination and arrogance like the evil of idolatry. Because you have rejected the word of the Lord, he has rejected you as king" (1 Samuel 15:22-23).

This was not the only time God showed disdain for pride. Perhaps the best example is not Saul, but Lucifer, a beautiful archangel. He thought of himself as equal to God and was cast out of heaven. When we make choices out of greed or selfish pride, we, too, will reap a whirlwind of God's judgement. Although we may not understand God's counsel or commands, we can be assured that He loves us and cares what happens to us. We may at times make mistakes, thinking we have done the right thing, as Saul did. But even though we fall short of the Father's expectations, we have a Great High Priest in Jesus Christ, who is ready to forgive us and intercede on our behalf. Through our humility and repentance before God we will experience His lavishing love and mercy.

Prayer: *O Lord, purge our hearts of anything that sets us against you. Convict us of our wrongs and pick us up again to do your will. In Jesus' name, Amen.*

A Closer Walk with God

Devotions from a Journey Through the Holy Lands

God Wins

View of the Valley of Jezreel from Megiddo

Mount Megiddo overlooks the fertile green Jezreel Valley. Many battles have been fought here, and over the centuries nations have thought they fought against heaven, because in each case God judged the best equipped and most successful armies. He exalted the humble in victory over false religions and superstitions.

Good triumphs over evil in the Valley of Jezreel. Consider King Ahab. He asked Naboth for his vineyard because it was near his palace, and he wanted to plant a vegetable garden there. Naboth shocked him when he stood up to the king. "The Lord forbid that I should give you the inheritance of my fathers" (1 Kings 21).

Ahab went home and pouted. His wife Jezebel asked him what was wrong, and he said Naboth would not sell him his vineyard. "Is this how a king behaves? Get up and eat. I will get the vineyard for you." She had Naboth killed and told her husband he could take possession of the land. Little good it did him. King Ahab died and the dogs licked up his blood. Jezebel died too, and the dogs devoured her. Since then, the name Jezebel has become a symbol of evil. In the book of Revelation, the name Jezebel is associated with women, both powerful and evil.

Armageddon, the final world war, will be fought in the Jezreel Valley. It will close the time of the Great Tribulation. Satan will make his final effort to oppose God's ultimate plan, but Jesus will return to rule on earth from the New Jerusalem.

God's people who face ridicule and persecution can be encouraged. We know from reading the book of Revelation that God wins the final battle. The blasphemers, mockers and persecutors will not be able to stand against the almighty God. They will have their place in hell for rejecting God's word, His power and His presence in this world.

Prayer: *Heavenly Father, as we see many of the signs of the end times told about in the Bible, help us not to be afraid, but to look forward to living with you forever. Help us to watch and prepare for your coming. Make us bold. Help us stand apart from the crowd and show your wonderful works to a lost and dying world. In Jesus' name. Amen.*

Extravagant Love

Downtown Nazareth

Nazareth is a bustling city—sounds of traffic, sites of street vendors, shops—not what I expected from reading the Bible. I looked for a village and found a reproduction of the ancient little town where Jesus grew up on a side street. Goats and donkeys made their way through crowded paths. I stood in a large upper room and imagined dirt falling when four men moved mud and reeds to lower their friend down on a mat in front of Jesus (Matthew 9). Caught off guard by such mercy, the crumbles of dirt falling in my hair didn't bother me. It was as if I heard Jesus say, "Son, your sins are forgiven," and, "Rise, take up your mat and walk." Jesus healed the crippled man based on the faith of his friends. He was a lucky man to experience the extravagant love of his friends.

This is the love that changes people. It changed me. Hurrying to meet my deadlines, I fell at work on a Friday afternoon and didn't know at the time that the fall broke my hip. When I couldn't get up, my friend Shirley asked me why I cried. "I'm afraid," I said.

Shirley surprised me when she laid down next to me, stretched out her arm and said, "You rest your head here and don't worry." She stayed on the floor with me until the ambulance came, and later she visited me in the hospital. Shirley was like the four friends of the paralytic when she took time out of her busy day and resisted being embarrassed to comfort me. She allowed God's extravagant love to flow through her. Since the accident, Shirley's sacrificial act has inspired me to find ways, even on busy days, to respond to the needs of others—opening doors for people in wheelchairs, giving a smile to a stressed cashier clerk in the grocery store or visiting someone who is confined to their home or hospital room.

Prayer: *Thank you, Lord for your extravagant love and for those who allow it to flow through them to us. Teach us to be more like them. In Jesus' name, Amen.*

The Lord is With You

A painting of the angel talking to Mary at the Basilica of the Annunciation, donated by the Philippines

The one good spring in all of Nazareth is certain to be the one that filled the well, which Mary drew water from. The Basilica of the Annunciation in the Greek Orthodox Church of St. Gabriel is built over the place where the angel Gabriel visited Mary. He said, "Greetings, you are highly favored! The Lord is with you."

The angel startled Mary. He said, "Do not be afraid, Mary, you have found favor with God. You will be with child and give birth to a son, and you are to give him the name Jesus. He will be great and will be called the Son of the Most High. The Lord God will give him the throne of his father David, and he will reign over the house of Jacob forever, his kingdom will never end" (Luke 1:30-33). Gabriel went on to explain how the Holy Spirit would come upon Mary and the Most High would overshadow her. Mary responded, "I am the Lord's servant. May it be to me as you have said" (Luke1:38).

Mary did not resist the angel's message. Neither did she fill with pride to be chosen by God to carry His son. She was a humble maid servant, ready to let Christ be born in her. I wonder how many times on the road to Bethlehem or during pregnancy Mary grew tired or frightened and remembered the words of Gabriel: "The Lord is with you." When we allow Christ to be born in our hearts, we can remember these words too. Times in this world when circumstances might cause us to be anxious, we can be assured that God is with us. One of His names, Emanuel, means "God with us."

Prayer: *Thank you Lord, for Mary's example of humility. Thank you for the peace that comes each day knowing you are with us. Help us to respond as Mary did, and follow the plan you have for us. In Jesus' name, Amen.*

Mighty God

Head waters of the Jordan River

The Jordan, the largest river in Israel, begins with the snow melt on Mount Hermon and is fed by springs and tributaries. It goes through the Sea of Galilee and descends nearly 1400 feet in elevation into the Dead Sea, the lowest place on earth. It is 150 miles long, which hardly compares with rivers like the Mississippi, 2,320 miles, the Missouri, 2,341, the Nile, 4,258 miles or the Amazon, 4,345 miles.

Perhaps it is not the river that is mighty, like we would expect from reading the Bible, but it is the mighty acts God performed along the river. Forty years after God delivered the Israelites from the Egyptians and parted the Red Sea, they stood on the banks of the Jordan River, which was at flood stage. Had God made a mistake? No! Joshua held his staff over the water and at that moment the priests who carried the ark stepped out in faith and their feet touched the waters' edge, the water upstream stopped. It piled up at a town called Adam and the people crossed the river on dry land.

Jacob wrestled with God at a ford near the Jabbok River, a tributary of the Jordan River, and this is where his name changed to Israel (Genesis 32:28). God took 300 fighting men with Gideon and defeated the Midianites (Judges 7:24). Elijah used his cloak to part the Jordan River so he and Elisha walked across on dry land. After Elijah was taken up in a chariot of fire, Elisha used his cloak to part the waters again so he could cross the river on dry land (2 Kings 2:12-14).

Covered with leprosy, Naaman went to Elisha who told him to wash seven times in the Jordan. Not impressed, Naaman walked away angry because he thought Elisha would call on the name of his God to heal him. But when Naaman changed his mind and did as the prophet said, his flesh was restored and became clean like that of a young boy (2 Kings 5:14).

The most memorable event on the Jordan River was when John the Baptist baptized our Savior, Jesus Christ. He walked out of the water and heaven opened. The Spirit of God descended on Him as a dove. From there Jesus went into the wilderness for forty days and forty nights where He was tested by the devil. I believe the words the Father spoke at Jesus' baptism: "This is my son, whom I love. With him I am well pleased" (Matthew 3:16-17) encouraged Him during the terrible time in the desert and helped Him to begin His earthly ministry.

The Israelites did not want to forget God's power demonstrated along the Jordan River. They set up stone monuments as memorials and told their children and grandchildren what God had done. Because of their special care to record these events along the Jordan River, we can read and experience the mighty works of God today.

As God's followers, it is good for us to set up memorials or write down times God has worked in our lives. These are things we can to talk about and celebrate. During times of trouble, we can find comfort as we remember what God has done for us in the past.

Prayer: *Thank you, Lord God, for memorials like the Jordan River. Help us to remember events in our own lives when you have shown us your mighty acts of love and mercy. In Jesus' name, Amen.*

A Closer Walk with God

The Chief Cornerstone

Outside the Church of St. Joseph

North of St. Gabriel's church is the Church of St. Joseph, also known as the Church of the Carpenter Shop. It is said to be built above Joseph's carpenter shop. We have understood the Greek word "tekton" to be "carpenter." However, the correct translation is *stone builder*. When we use this translation, many passages in Scripture come to life as they reflect on Jesus' life. He used construction metaphors in his teaching. Jesus said in the Sermon on the Mount, "Everyone who hears these words of mine and puts them into practice is like a wise man who built his house on the rock. The rain came down, the streams rose, and the winds blew and beat against the house; yet it did not fall, because it had its foundation on the rock. But everyone who hears these words of mine and does not put them into practice is like a foolish man who built his house on sand.

The rain came down, the streams rose, and the winds blew and beat against the house and it fell with a great crash" (Matthew 7:24-27).

Jesus referred to Himself when He said in Matthew 21:42: "The stone the builders rejected has become the capstone (cornerstone); The Lord has done this, and it is marvelous in our eyes."

Paul said, "Consequently, you are no longer foreigners and aliens, but fellow citizens with God's people and members of God's household, built on the foundation of the apostles and prophets, with Christ Jesus himself as the chief cornerstone. In him the whole building is joined together and rises to become a holy temple in the Lord" (Ephesians 2:19-22).

Peter said, "As you come to him, the living Stone—rejected by men but chosen by God and precious to him—you also, like living stones, are being built into a spiritual house to be a holy priesthood, offering spiritual sacrifices acceptable to God through Jesus Christ" (1 Peter 2:4-5).

The following are fulfillment of Old Testament verses:

"From Judah will come the cornerstone" (Zechariah 10:4) and "See, I lay a stone in Zion (Jerusalem), a tested stone, a precious cornerstone for a sure foundation; the one who relies on it will never be dismayed. I will make justice the measuring line and righteousness the plumb line" (Isaiah 28:16).

In Europe and America many buildings are made from wood construction, and it is easy for us to think of Jesus as a carpenter, a person who works with wood. However, buildings in Israel are made from limestone and basalt. It makes more sense that Joseph and Jesus were stone cutters. The father and the Son worked together in Nazareth on local construction projects. The Father and the Son work together today to build a firm foundation of our faith. Jesus is our Cornerstone. Let's let Him align our relationship with God and our relationship(s) with others.

Prayer: *Holy God, help us to break through our traditional thinking to understand how you lived and what you said from your life to illustrate the truth about why you came. Make us into your Holy Temple until you come again. In Christ Jesus, Amen.*

The Gates of Hell

The Gates of Hell

"When Jesus came to the region of Caesarea Philippi, he asked his disciples, 'Who do people say the Son of Man is?'

"They replied, 'Some say John the Baptist; others say Elijah; and still others, Jeremiah or one of the prophets.'

"But what about you?" he asked. "who do you say I am?"

"Simon Peter answered, 'You are the Christ, the Son of the living God.'

"Jesus replied, 'Blessed are you, Simon son of Jonah, for this was not revealed to you by man, but by my Father in heaven. And I tell you that you are Peter, and on this rock I will build my church, and the gates of Hades (Hell) will not overcome it'" (Matthew 16:13-18).

Caesarea Philippi is located near Dan, a paradise of beautiful pools and lush woods at the head waters of the Jordan River. Set on the russet cliffs of Mt. Hermon, a rock-hewn cave has stood for thousands of years. To the ancient people, this cave was known as "The Gates of Hades (Hell)." The large dark opening of the cave was the scene of human sacrifice where people were thrown and never seen again.

Could the disciples have thought that Jesus would build his church at the location of this rock-hewn cave at the base of Mt. Hermon? Nothing is impossible for God! A second interpretation of this Scripture might be that the name Peter means "rock," and Jesus would use Peter to preach the gospel, which He did.

However, the most accepted interpretation of the Scripture is that the "rock" is Peter's confession about who Jesus is—the Messiah, the Savior of our souls—why He came to earth, worked as a servant, suffered, died and rose from the dead for our forgiveness and eternal life. Jesus experienced every temptation, trial and suffering that we do, and more, but He did not sin. He is our Great High Priest who understands our predicament, loves us and wants to be in a relationship with us.

The world today can be quite confusing with all its religions, weird ideas and beliefs. Some things people say make sense, but we will only know the truth if we read God's word to learn about His character and His will for our lives. He wants to take away our confusion. He wants to be our Friend.

Thank you, Lord, for vivid pictures in your word that translate the truth about you and why you came, and why you want to be with us forever. Make us aware of your presence with us every day. In Jesus' name, Amen.

Try Again

4,000-year-old city gate at Hazor

Hazor was the largest and one of the most important Canaanite cities in the Old Testament. It was located eight miles north of the Sea of Galilee on a major international road from Egypt to Phoenicia and Assyria. The tel that stands today is 130 feet high with over 23 layers of cities. In 2014, archaeologists uncovered a huge city gate, more than 4,000 years old, which means Abraham walked through that gate.

Joshua defeated and burned Hazor and other Canaanite cities (Joshua 11:1-11). The Canaanites resettled the ruins of Hazor, but Deborah and Barak defeated it again (Judges 4:1-24). Solomon fortified the city (1 Kings 9:15), and it served as a military supply depot and administrative center under the Israelite kings Omri and Ahab. They built administration buildings, storehouses, palaces and a water supply system. Later Hazor was destroyed by fire and after the fire by an earthquake.

Even though God had given this city to His people, they were not successful at overcoming the Canaanites. Their victories were temporary. We can find spiritual parallels in our personal lives to the Israelite struggles. Sometimes the enemy we thought we overcame—a temptation, thought pattern, or a bad habit re-enters our lives and we wonder why.

Christians have been warned many times to remain strong in their faith and not to return to their previous sins. But how can we fight this aggressive enemy? Paul said to the Corinthians that "the weapons we fight with are not the weapons of the world. On the contrary, they have divine power to demolish strongholds" (2 Corinthians 10:4), and "No temptation has seized you except what is common to man. And God is faithful; he will not let you be tempted beyond what you can bear. But when you are tempted, he will also provide a way out so that you can stand up under it" (1 Corinthians 10:13).

Paul also taught the Ephesians to put on the full armor of God: "Stand firm then, with the belt of truth buckled around your waist, with the breastplate of righteousness in place, and with your feet fitted with the readiness that comes from the gospel of peace. In addition to all this, take up the shield of faith, with which you can extinguish all the flaming arrows of the evil one. Take the helmet of salvation and the sword of the Spirit, which is the word of God. And pray in the Spirit on all occasions" (Ephesians 6:14-18).

Hazor may remind us how vulnerable we are to temptation and sin, but God is bigger than any of our enemies. We can be comforted knowing He is always with us.

Prayer: *Thank you, Lord, for teaching us to be prepared against the sin that so easily entangles our lives. Thank you for weapons we can use in our spiritual battles and help us fight our enemy, the devil. In Jesus' name, Amen.*

God's Judgement

A nature preserve at the head waters of the Jordan River in Dan

The name Dan means "judge." It didn't seem like an appropriate name to me as I walked through the nature preserve of ancient oaks, pistachio trees and a thick tangled jungle at the headwaters of the Jordan River. Fed by springs, waterfalls and the snow melt of Mt. Hermon, Tel Dan is often referred to as Israel's Garden of Eden. The spies returned to Moses from this paradise and said, "It is a good land that the Lord our God is giving us" (Deuteronomy 1:25), but the Israelites were afraid to take the land because of the Amorites. They settled Dan, and Moses said to them, "The Lord himself goes before you and will be with you; he will never leave you nor forsake you. Do not be afraid; do not be discouraged" (Deuteronomy 31:8). Yet the Israelites who settled there chose their ways instead of God's ways.

Jonathan, a Levite, became the priest of Dan. He set up an image stolen from Micah's house in Ephraim (Judges 18). Known as a center for cults, it is no mystery that Dan was destroyed by the Arameans and later by the Syrians.

Jeremiah warned that further destruction was coming: "A voice is announcing from Dan, proclaiming disaster from the hills of Ephraim. 'Tell this to the nations, proclaim it to Jerusalem: 'A besieging army is coming from a distant land raising war against the cities of Judah. They surround her like men guarding a field, because she has rebelled against me,' declares the Lord" (Jeremiah 4:15-16). Although Jeremiah warned God's people, they refused to listen and were defeated. This was the last mention of Dan in the Bible.

The destruction of Dan may seem unmerciful, but could it be an act of grace? Solomon wrote in Proverbs 3:11-12, "My son, do not despise the Lord's discipline and do not resent his rebuke, because the Lord disciplines those he loves as a father the son he delights in."

Dan's people who lived in this paradise did not accept God's grace, and the city of Dan became a symbol of judgment. "No discipline seems pleasant at the time, but painful" (Hebrews 12:11). God's judgment and discipline are prominent themes in the prophets' messages. Let them remind us of a God who loves and wants to be our Friend. What He expects in return is for us to love Him and each other—not other gods or idols.

Thank you, Father God, for grace through discipline. Help us to learn your ways by listening to your words written in the Bible, spoken through willing servants and prompted by the Holy Spirit. In Jesus' name, Amen.

Mountain of Majesty

Mt. Hermon, Israel – Photo by Amit erez

Mount Hermon, a limestone mountain with an elevation over 9,000 feet, is located in northern Israel. Snow-capped the year-round, it has meadows as green as emeralds, clear water ponds and vibrant hills flooded with red, pink, white and yellow wild flowers. Thirty miles long with three large peaks, Mount Hermon seems more like a mountain range than a single mountain. Pine forests, fruit and almond orchards cover the lower slopes.

Several groups over the centuries have considered the mountain sacred. Archaeologists have surveyed more than twenty temples, many of which seem to be Canaanite or Phoenician cult centers where Baal Shamaim (Lord of the Heavens) might have been worshipped.

It was on this mountain where Jesus led Peter, James and John to witness His transfiguration. His face shone like the sun, and his clothes gleamed the purest white. He talked with Moses and Elijah.

So awed was Peter by the experience, he volunteered to build three shrines—one for Moses, one for Elijah, and one for Jesus. While the words were still on his tongue, a bright cloud overshadowed them and a voice spoke from it. "This is my son whom I love. With him I am well pleased. Listen to him!" (Matthew 17:5). This terrified the disciples and they fell on their faces. Jesus reached down and touched them. "Don't be afraid," He said. When they looked up, they only saw Jesus.

Although it took time for Peter to process what happened on the mountain, he testified of it in his ministry. He said, "We were eyewitnesses of his majesty. He received honor and glory from God the Father, when a voice came to him from the Majestic Glory, saying, 'This is my son whom I love . . .' We ourselves heard this voice that came from heaven when we were with him on the sacred mountain" (2 Peter 1:16-17).

I am a lot like Peter—still processing my journey through Israel. Whatever trail you are on, take time to ponder, discuss and relive mountain top experiences. Consider how God may want you to use it for His glory.

Prayer: *Thank you, Lord, for the opportunity to walk in the land where you walked and to see the things you saw. Thank you for opening up your stories so we can see your word more clearly. Send your Holy Spirit on each of us to understand and apply your will in our lives. In Christ Jesus, Amen.*

Jesus' Hometown

Capernaum, where Jesus called home

Resting on the northern shore of the Sea of Galilee is the fishing town of Capernaum, the focal point of Jesus' ministry. Vibrant pink, purple and crimson bougainvillea, green eucalyptus and palm trees speak of the fertile soil and mild climate. Peter, Andrew, Philip, James and John—five of the twelve disciples—were from nearby Bethsaida. Jesus called Capernaum home—not Bethlehem where

He was born; not Nazareth where He grew up and not Jerusalem, the religious center for Israel.

It was in Capernaum where Jesus healed Peter's mother-in-law, the paralytic man, the man possessed by demons, the centurion's servant, the woman with an issue of blood and where He raised Jairus' daughter from the dead.

Jesus used the miracles to show people He was the Messiah, to authenticate His message and draw attention to His teaching. The purpose in all He did was to inspire changed lives.

Peter got it. After Jesus' resurrection, he healed a crippled beggar at the temple gate called Beautiful. Peter responded to the man's request for money. "Silver or gold I do not have, but what I have I give you. In the name of Jesus Christ of Nazareth, walk." Taking him by the right hand, he helped him up, and instantly the man's feet and ankles became strong. He jumped to his feet and began to walk. Then he went with them into the temple courts, walking and jumping, and praising God" (Acts 3:1-8). Peter used the attention from the miracle as an opportunity to preach the message, as Jesus would have preached it: "Repent, then, and turn to God, so that your sins may be wiped out, that times of refreshing may come from the Lord" (Acts 3:19).

However, the teaching and miracles Jesus performed did not bring repentance. "Then Jesus began to denounce the towns in which most of his miracles had been performed, because their lives did not change. "Woe to you, Chorazin! Woe to you, Bethsaida! For if the miracles that were performed in you had been performed in Tyre and Sidon, they would have repented long ago in sackcloth and ashes. But I tell you, it will be more bearable for Tyre and Sidon on the day of judgment than for you. And you, Capernaum, will you be lifted to the heavens? No, you will go down to Hades, for if the miracles that were performed in you had been performed in Sodom, it would have remained to this day. But I tell you that it will be more bearable for Sodom on the day of judgment than for you" (Matthew 11:20-24).

It would be easy for us to read about the miracles and wonder why the people did not respond. Instead, let us focus on Jesus and become more deeply convinced that He is who He said, the Son of God. And like Peter, let us devote our lives to telling others about Him, His forgiveness and the eternal life He offers to those who believe. Someone needs to hear it today. People experience fear, anxiety, loss of loved ones and loss of health or wealth. They need hope, peace, joy and strength to face tomorrow. Their deepest need is knowing Jesus as their Friend and Savior.

O Lord, make us beacons of your light and love to the nations. Be our confidence and peace as we reach out to a dying world. Help us show love and compassion as Jesus would. In His great name, Amen.

Ruins of old Capernaum

A Closer Walk with God

Quiet! Be Still!

A party boat on the Sea of Galilee

The Sea of Galilee is a sapphire blue, freshwater lake in the shape of a harp. It is often called Yam Kinneret, which means "harp" in Hebrew. Surrounded by golden mountains and lush green plains, the area attracts both farmers and fishermen.

The Sea of Galilee is fed by the Jordan River, Mount Hermon's snow melt and hot water springs. It is 12.5 miles long, 7 miles wide and is 700 feet below sea level. Although Jesus performed many miracles around the lake, it has two distinct sides—a Jewish side and a Gentile side, which answers a life-long question for me: *Why would a herd of pigs be in Israel?* The miracle of pigs dashing down a cliff did not happen on the Jewish side.

From April through November a gentle morning breeze flows from the west and picks up in the afternoon. From December through March, however, the winds are unpredictable. This must have been the time of the year when Jesus got into the boat with His disciples. He probably fell asleep in the back under a restful rocking of the boat. A furious squall rose and water broke over the sides and nearly swamped the boat. The disciples, who were experienced fishermen, panicked. "Don't you care if we drown?" they said to Jesus. Then Jesus stood and said to the wind and waves, "Quiet! Be Still!" This terrified the men even more. "Who is this? Even the wind and waves obey Him" (Mark 4:37-41).

I spent a memorable birthday in April on the Sea of Galilee. The morning breeze had grown stronger, but the boat was big and strong. I was not afraid. The captain turned on lively music and led us in happy circle dances. Later when I had time to process the afternoon, I realized that this lake was where Jesus preached and healed the sick. He delivered a man from demons and cast his legion of demons into a herd of pigs that jumped off a cliff and into the lake below (Mark 5). He healed two blind men (Matthew 9:27-31) and preached from a boat slightly off shore to the people along the water's edge.

The places Jesus preached and healed people were out in the countryside and along the lake—not in convenient air conditioned buildings. He used fearful circumstances to demonstrate His power over the things that make us anxious. As He calmed the wind and waves of the sea, He can quiet our fears. He is always with us. He has power over creation; power over sin and death; and power over our problems. We can trust Him to walk with us—comfort and counsel us.

Prayer: *O Lord, help us to be still and know that you are God and that you love us. Thank you for always being with us no matter what our circumstances are. In Jesus' name, Amen.*

Jesus' Greatest Sermon

Church at the Mount of Beatitudes

Between Tabgha and Capernaum is the Mount of Beatitudes, the place where Jesus preached His most important message. Green meadows, towering trees and bright colored flowers make the Mount of Beatitudes a heavenly showplace. Birds seem to sing of God's glory. Franciscans built a modern church on the hilltop—not over the ruins of an ancient Byzantine church. Along the grounds surrounding the modern church are monuments inscribed with the words of each blessing in this passage of Scripture. Inside the new octagonal church structure, each wall is inscribed with the same blessings.

When Jesus saw the crowds, he went up on this mountainside and sat down. His disciples came to him, and He began to teach them what it meant to be blessed (rich) in God's kingdom. God created His people to be dependent on Him, not earthly wealth. The Sermon on the Mount, called the Beatitudes, is Jesus' message of hope and joy, independent of outward circumstances. Jesus says in Matthew 5, 6 and 7 that "what we do" speaks louder than "what we say."

Jesus' heart for His people is in this message. When we are down, He encourages us. When we are sad, He comforts us. He desires humility over pride or arrogance and says the meek (not the weak) will inherit the earth. Jesus says when we hunger and thirst for more of Him, more truth, more righteousness, we will be filled. When we show mercy to others, He will show mercy to us. God loves the pure in heart. Who could that be? A child? Let us be like children—pure and dependent on God. Jesus did not promise us an easy street to Heaven. He talked about persecution. But He said He would always be with us, even as He stood with Stephen when he was stoned (Acts 7:54-60).

We serve a loving and merciful God, who wants us to experience His power at work in us. We may get overwhelmed by our circumstances, but God is with us. Nothing is impossible for Him. He has done great things in others, and He will do great things in us when we trust Him with all our hearts.

Prayer: *Thank you, Lord, for teaching us what is most important. Help us to live the way you want us to live—to show love and mercy, to be kind and generous, to be more like Jesus. In His name, we pray, Amen.*

The Beatitudes

Blessed are the poor in spirit, for theirs is the kingdom of heaven.
Blessed are those who mourn, for they will be comforted.
Blessed are the meek, for they will inherit the earth.
Blessed are those who hunger and thirst for righteousness, for they will be filled.
Blessed are the merciful, for they will be shown mercy.
Blessed are the pure in heart, for they will be called sons of God.
Blessed are those who are persecuted because of righteousness, for theirs is the kingdom of heaven.
Matthew 5:1-9

A Closer Walk with God

A Boy's Offering

Inside the Church of the Multiplication of the Loaves and Fishes

The Church of the Multiplication of the Loaves and Fishes is in Tabgha, ancient Heptapegon, on the northwest shore of the Sea of Galilee. The modern church stands on the site of fourth and fifth century churches.

Flowing fountains create a peaceful reverence, and tourists hush their chatter in front of the altar. Above the altar is a mosaic of five loaves and two fishes. The floors are artistic mosaic tile. The miracle of the loaves and fishes is a reminder that God takes our offerings, no matter how large or small, and multiplies them for His purposes. Imagine a boy's delight to see how God used his lunch to feed thousands (John 6:1-15). What if we, like the boy, willingly gave what we had for God's use. Maybe we, too, would be surprised to see Him at work in our lives.

I once knew a couple who tested 2 Corinthians 9:7: "Each man should give what he has decided in his heart to give, not reluctantly or under compulsion, for God loves a cheerful giver." Instead of giving the suggested 10%, they cheerfully gave 50% of their income. They learned, like the young boy, that God increased their blessing so they could keep giving. The final result was what the couple called hilarious giving.

The subject of giving has been a stumbling block for many believers. However, God loved us so much He *gave* His only Son for the forgiveness of our sins. He honored the boy's gift with a miracle. He gave tribute to a widow in the temple for her small gift of two copper coins (Mark 12:42). He defended Mary, Lazarus' sister when she anointed His feet with expensive perfume (John 12:1-8). Are we ready to serve God and others—to give our time, talents and money; to show mercy, love and compassion to follow Jesus' examples?

Prayer: *O Lord, teach us to be wise with our blessings—how we spend and save money. Help us to be generous as you have been generous with us. In Jesus' name, Amen.*

Village by the Sea

A first century fishing boat

Magdala, a fishing village once located between the cliffs of Mount Arbel and the Sea of Galilee, is the hometown of Mary Magdalene, a woman who Jesus cast out seven demons, one of the women at His crucifixion, and the first person to see the resurrected Christ.

Because of the changes in sea level over the centuries, the piers, warehouses and markets were submerged in the lake. The town owed its prosperity to agriculture and the fishing industry. In January 1986, due to years of drought, when the water level of the Sea of Galilee was extremely low, two brothers in the local kibbutz found the outline of a boat in the mud. When it was excavated, archaeologists determined it to be a first century fishing boat. Preserved in a special chemical solution, this "Jesus boat" is on display at the Kubbutz Ginnosar museum on the site of ancient Magdala. I imagined what it was like when Jesus was in this place.

After He had spent three days with a crowd of more than four thousand and fed them, He got into a boat, like the one in the picture, and went to the area of Magadan. Some Pharisees and Sadducees came to test Him by asking Him to give them a sign from heaven. Jesus called them a wicked and adulterous generation and said they would get no sign except that of Jonah. He referred to His own death and resurrection, which would happen in the near future (Matthew 16:1-4). Some of the leaders in Magdala also asked Jesus for a sign. This was where Jesus' miracles were well known. What more did they want?

During the time John the Baptist was in prison, he sent one of his disciples to ask Jesus if He was the expected Messiah. Jesus said, "Go back and report to John what you hear and see: The blind receive their sight, the lame walk, those who have leprosy are cured, the deaf hear, the dead are raised, the good news is preached to the poor. Blessed is the man who does not fall away on account of me" (Matthew 11:4-6). These verses are fulfillment of Isaiah 35:5-6: "Then will the eyes of the blind be opened and the ears of the deaf unstopped. Then will the lame leap like deer and the mute tongue shout for joy."

Jesus pointed out to the religious leaders in Magdala that the miracles He performed were proof enough of who He was, the Son of God. Blinded by what they expected the Messiah to be, they missed their Savior. The religious leaders thought the Christ would free them from Roman oppression, but He came to set them free from sin so they could be in relationship with Him and live forever.

Jesus our Savior is not what people expect today. They don't understand how a loving God could allow terror and suffering in this world. They judge Him on their standards and hang on to fear, anger, anxiety and bitterness, when they could experience God's lavishing love, peace, hope and eternal life by accepting who He says He is.

Prayer: *O Lord, send your Spirit to break through the barriers people erect against you because they do not understand what it means to live in a sinful world with a loving God. Shine your light and love through us so they might see a glimpse of you and turn to experience your amazing love. In Jesus' name, Amen.*

Obedience Matters to God

Today's Jericho

Jericho is a lush green oasis eighteen miles east of Jerusalem in a barren white valley. It is 812 feet below sea level, which makes it the lowest city on earth. Palms, citrus, banana and balsam trees grow in this natural hot house. The only evidence of the ancient city, the walls that fell at the sound of the Israelites' loud shout, is a mud brick mound and a portion of the northern wall, which was where Rahab lived. A city tower from 7000 B.C. also lies in a trench near the tel.

Jericho was the first city to be defeated by the Israelites as they entered the Promised Land. I questioned, *could a loud shout cause walls six feet deep and in some places twenty feet deep and twenty feet high to fall*? Jericho was tightly shut up because of the Israelites (Joshua 6). This was a people whose God rescued them from slavery in Egypt and parted the Red Sea so they could walk across on dry land. As soon as the Israelites crossed, the waters covered the

Egyptian army, horses and chariots. *What would the people of Jericho have felt as the Israelites marched around the city every day for six days*? On the seventh day God instructed them to march around the city seven times. At the sound of a trumpet blast the people gave a loud shout and the walls fell.

As strange as the instructions were, the Israelites obeyed. They had complained and disobeyed many times in the wilderness and suffered for it. This time they did exactly what God said. It was God who caused the walls to fall. Nothing that the people did—not the marching or the shouting. It was because the Israelites did what God instructed them to do that He delivered Jericho into their hands.

The New Testament has a key story of Jesus being in Jericho. I wondered if Zacchaeus was familiar with the two-thousand-year-old history of Jericho? He was not a believer when Jesus entered Jericho. Yet, he was a curious man, and since he was not very tall, he climbed up in a sycamore tree so he could see Jesus. When Jesus saw him, He said, "Zacchaeus, come down immediately. I must stay at your house today" (Luke 19:5). The little man came down the tree and rushed to his house to meet the Lord. This was a turning point in Zacchaeus' life. Everyone in the city hated him because he was a tax collector. Like most tax collectors, he was dishonest and gouged people for more money than the government required. He kept the surplus for himself. Jesus changed all that when he showed love and respect to Zacchaeus. The tax collector repaid the people he had cheated four times the amount, and he gave half of his possessions to the poor.

The road from Jerusalem to Jericho is rocky and treacherous. The Good Samaritan traveled this road and found a man left for dead by robbers and nursed his wounds. He asked an innkeeper to care for him in his absence (Luke 10:30-35). The Bible does not record that God gave the Samaritan instructions about what to do. Did he do it out of the goodness of his heart? I choose to believe that he exhibited the fruit of the Spirit—love, joy, peace, patience, kindness, goodness, faithfulness, gentleness and self-control (Galatians 5:22-23). He could not leave the battered man on the road to die because he possessed the nature of God within him.

Like Joshua and the Israelites, Zacchaeus, or the Good Samaritan, we can choose God's ways over our own selfish, self-centered lifestyles. We can stand out and make a difference in people's lives or go with the flow of every-man-for-himself.

Prayer: *Holy Father, make us aware of the needs of others. In each situation, help us to know how to love as you do and obey your will in our lives. In Jesus' name, Amen.*

A Closer Walk with God

Devotions from a Journey Through the Holy Lands

God's Meeting Place

The women's portion of the Western (Wailing)
Wall beyond the Dome of The Rock

Israeli soldiers and the Arab Temple Mount Police guard what may be the most revered place on earth, the Dome of the Rock. It was built on the foundation of the temple mount constructed by King Solomon, which was and is over the place where Abraham was willing to sacrifice Isaac, his son (2 Chronicles 3:1). Behind the temple and in a large courtyard, some stones on the Western Wall are up to ten feet high and nearly forty-five feet long. These stones are incredible to see; even more amazing to mentally process how they got there. The Western Wall is a place where Jews and Christians pray. I visited an underground part of the wall where women pray. There in the narrow tunnel I wrote my requests on a small piece of paper—naming each person in my family and tucked it between two large stones.

The temple has been destroyed several times, but when Herod rebuilt it, his workmen spent eight years quarrying and shaping the stones for the walls. It is the temple Herod constructed where Mary and Joseph brought Jesus when He was eight days old. It was here that Simeon prayed, "Sovereign Lord, as you have promised, you now dismiss your servant in peace. For my eyes have seen your salvation, which you have prepared in the sight of all people, a light for revelation to the Gentiles for the glory to your people Israel" (Luke 2:29-32). This is also where the prophetess Anna gave thanks to God and proclaimed the future redemption of Jerusalem through Jesus (Luke 2:36). This is the temple where Mary and Joseph found twelve-year-old Jesus listening to the priests and asking questions three days after the Passover (Luke 2:41). It's the place where Jesus overturned the tables of the moneychangers (Matthew 21:12, Mark 11:15-17, and John 2:14-16). Jesus spent much time here teaching and performing miracles.

While the Dome of the Rock is overlaid with gold and is regarded as the meeting place of God, Jesus purchased our immediate access to the Father with His own blood on the cross. The earth shook and the curtain in the most holy place in the temple was torn in two, top to bottom. All barriers to God were broken down.

As craftsmen took many years to build and rebuild the temple throughout history, God is building a church through His people. Peter said, "You are a chosen people, a royal priesthood, a holy nation, a people belonging to God, that you may declare the praises of him who called you out of darkness into his wonderful light" (1 Peter 2:9).

Hebrews 4:16 says: "Let us approach the throne of grace with confidence, so that we may receive mercy and find grace to help us in our time of need."

People today need to know about this clear access to a God who loves and cares about them. They need the comfort of His words, help in troubling times, and peace for their souls. God depends on His people to partner with Him by being where people meet God.

Devotions from a Journey Through the Holy Lands

Prayer: *O Lord, be born in us so we may be a people where others meet God. Empower us to love as you do, to show mercy, kindness and gentleness to others so they might see You in us and respond to You with their love. In Christ we pray, Amen.*

Herod's Beachfront Property

Ruins of an aqueduct, which carried water from Mt. Hermon to Caesarea

    Although Herod the Great had many palaces, he poured all his creativity into the palace at Caesarea. Ruins of elaborate dining halls and estate rooms are on the beach of the eastern shores of the Mediterranean Sea. A line of arches supported a massive aqueduct system where water flowed from Mount Hermon to the sea. Near the harbor in full view of the sea is a theater where horse races were held, and an amphitheater, which seated 4,000 guests. Herod dedicated this magnificent city, built entirely of limestone, to Caesar Augustus. For 600 years Caesarea, not Jerusalem, was the capital of Judea.

    Cornelius, a Roman centurion who feared God and gave to the poor, lived in Caesarea, a gentile city. Until this time only Jews were Christians. It may surprise many to know that Jesus, His disciples and the first converts were devout Jews. They proclaimed the good news about forgiveness and eternal life through the death and resurrection of Jesus Christ. Cornelius sent to Joppa for Peter, and he came to Caesarea. He said to him, "You are well aware that it is against our law for a Jew to associate with a gentile or visit him. But God has shown me that I should not call any man impure or unclean" (Acts 10:28).

The conversion of Cornelius, the first gentile Christian, was a pivotal point in Christian history. This was not just any gentile. He was an officer in the Roman army, which occupied Israel. This was not any ordinary gentile city, but the most pagan and dedicated to Caesar and the worship of Rome. God made the point that gentiles would be included in the covenant of God's people and such inclusion crossed political boundaries. Ironically, God chose a city of Jewish-gentile conflict to be the launching point of his mission to unite all people.

Gentile Christians were once strangers to God's covenant. It is by grace that we have been admitted into a relationship with the Father through Jesus. Paul said, "This mystery is that through the gospel the gentiles are heirs together with Israel, members together of one body, and sharers together in the promise in Christ Jesus" (Ephesians 3:6). He also said, "If some of the branches have been broken off, and you, though a wild olive shoot, have been grafted in among the others and now share in the nourishing sap from the olive root, do not boast over those branches. If you do, consider this: You do not support the root, but the root supports you" (Romans 11:17-18).

We share a great inheritance in the Kingdom of God. God has no prejudice, no favorites. We are all precious in His sight, saved by the blood of Jesus, set free from sin, death and Satan.

Prayer: *Father God, thank you that you accept all who believe in the Lord Jesus, His death and resurrection for our forgiveness and eternal life. Help us to lose our prejudice and grow to be more like Jesus. In His great name, Amen.*

A Time of Blessing

A young woman plays the harp in a passage way near the City of David.

People pushed their way into the Church of the Holy Sepulchre. It was so crowded I could hardly move one way or the other. Fear of getting separated from my friends was intense. My head screamed in pain. Once out of the church, our group met in a nearby outdoor café for lunch. My headache persisted.

Then we walked down a narrow passage. I heard a heavenly melody from a harp and sat down on a short stone wall of a tree planter. I closed my eyes. The music relaxed me and soothed my stress. I opened my eyes and was glad to see my travel buddies around me. I asked them where the music came from. They pointed. I walked a few steps in that direction. A young woman played the harp. Behind her was a golden statue of David playing his harp.

I knew in that moment why King Saul's servants called for a harpist to soothe the king's debilitating headaches. Someone in the palace knew about a shepherd boy named David. They called for him to come and play his harp for the king. From that time, whenever the disturbing spirit came on King Saul, David played his harp for him (1 Samuel 16:14-23).

Although Saul disobeyed, God had mercy on him. He sent David to play the harp and Saul's aching pain dissipated. In the same way God revived me. I spent the rest of the day seeing more of Jerusalem—walking on stone streets, enjoying the clanging of church bells, the chants of Jews and Muslims, visiting museums and shopping.

Prayer: *Thank you, Lord, for the harp music. It soothed my troubled soul and inspired me to move on to learn more about the city Jesus loved. In His name, Amen.*

A Mighty Fortress

A model of the Masada Fortress

Masada rose 1500 feet above the south shores of the Dead Sea, and was a natural fortress. Although King David used the mountain cliffs as a refuge, it was first developed by Jonathan, the Hasmonean ruler (161-143 B.C.). Herod the Great added more buildings to the fortress. His palace rested on three terraces at the edge of the western cliff. He used the large plateau for agricultural purposes and constructed huge rooms to store grain and produce. He had twelve cisterns quarried out of the rock on the northwest side of the cliff and filled them with water from the wadis of Masada. He also dug two large cisterns to fill with rain water. The elaborate water system supplied water for drinking, irrigation, a swimming pool and Roman baths. Herod strengthened the natural fortress with a double wall 4500 feet long, surrounding the top of the mountain. It had thirty towers and gates at the two paths that led into the stronghold.

Herod's extensive construction on this mountain revealed his great fear of running out of food and water in addition to his fear of enemy attacks. He depended on his own intelligence and wealth to overcome his anxieties. In contrast, David found a mighty fortress in God and used metaphors from this mountain to describe God. "The Lord is my rock, my fortress and my deliverer; my God is my rock, in whom I take refuge. He is my shield, and the horn of my salvation, my stronghold" (Psalm 18:2).

David knew his protection came from God and not Masada, which was thought to be resistant to enemy attacks. However, the Romans destroyed the beautiful fortress in 73 A.D. Jews living there at that time committed suicide rather than be tortured, enslaved or killed by the Romans. They left behind fragments of scrolls and a few books of the Bible, which included Genesis, Leviticus, Deuteronomy, Ezekiel and Psalms. A few of their names and messages were written on shards of broken pottery. Two women and three children hid during the Roman attack and lived. Historian Flavius Josephus also survived to write Roman and Biblical history.

Like Herod, people today suffer from fear and anxiety. They try to face fear in their own strength. The Bible records the words, "Do not be afraid," 365 times, proof that God knows our circumstances and wants us to trust Him and not to be afraid. Will we find a mighty fortress in our God or trust in our health, wealth, status, or power to save us from what makes us anxious?

Prayer: *Holy God, you are my fortress, my hiding place. Increase my faith and teach me to trust You as I face my fears. Thank you for your love and faithfulness. In Jesus' name, Amen.*

Love Your Enemies

One of the caves where the Dead Sea Scrolls were found

Sulphurous fumes from nearby hot springs, the glassiness of the Dead Sea, burning heat and treacherous cliffs make Qumran an unlikely place to choose to live. However, people have lived in the nearby mountain caves.

In 1946, Bedouin shepherd boys looking for lost sheep threw a stone into one of the caves. Shocked by a cracking sound, the boys returned the next day with their parents to see what was in the cave. They removed several jars, which contained scrolls, and took them to an antiquities dealer in Bethlehem who determined they were ancient manuscripts of the Bible.

In 1949, a search of the surrounding area of Qumran resulted in the discovery of more caves with manuscripts hidden in clay jars. Because of the dry climate, the documents were well preserved. All eleven caves held scrolls. The fourth cave held 15,000 fragments of 516 manuscripts. The Dead Sea Scrolls consisted of more than 800 different documents. Every book of the Old Testament was represented except the book of Esther. The only complete manuscript found was the book of Isaiah. Letters, hymns, prayers and books of community rules were included in the discoveries.

The people who lived in Qumran about the time of Jesus had beliefs similar to Judaism and Christianity. However, they believed that they were the elect people of God. Several writings explain the conditions for admittance to the community, requirements for living there and consequences for disobedience.

The differences in belief hardly make any connection to Christianity. The Essenes who lived in Qumran strictly adhered to rules regarding cleanliness and uncleanliness, Jesus didn't. He was also criticized for eating with sinners and tax collectors and healing on the Sabbath. The Essenes withdrawal to the stark unpleasant conditions of the desert might have something to do with their world view of loving their friends and hating their enemies.

In contrast, Jesus made a statement about this in the Sermon on the Mount. "You have heard that it was said, 'You shall love your neighbor and hate your enemy,' But I tell you: Love your enemies and pray for those who persecute you" (Matthew 5:43).

Prayer: *Thank you, Father God, for your faithfulness to be with us in all circumstances. Help us to pray for those who commit great evil against us. Help us to pray for the persecuted church—that you would shine your light and love through these people to save the worst of sinners. In Jesus' name, Amen.*

A Time of Testing

A monastery hidden between two mountains in the area where the Dead Sea Scrolls were found

The Israelites were tested in the Negev. I was too—the heat, the high mountain walks over rocky paths and the small dark hiding places. I wanted to go to the hotel—no more hiking. I was on information overload, tired, hot and irritable. My energy was zapped. My strength hung on threads.

God said, *WAIT!*

I got off the bus again to see a monastery hidden on a mountainside cliff. How was it possible to build in this place hundreds of years ago? I stood in the shade of a cross mount and listened to our guide. "This is the wilderness where John the Baptist lived and preached," she said. I wondered how anyone could live in this hot, dry desert.

Yet, people trudged through this parched land from towns near and far to see John the Baptist. Jesus said, "What did you go out into the wilderness to see? A reed swayed by the wind? If not, what did you go out to see? A man dressed in fine clothes? No, those who wear fine clothes are in kings' palaces. Then what did you go out to see? A prophet? Yes, I tell you, and more than a prophet" (Matthew 11:7-10).

John the Baptist was prophesied about in the book of Isaiah more than 700 years before he was born, and he fulfilled what was said about him—that he would prepare the way for the Lord. We can believe Scripture when it proves itself, and it does over and over again.

My time of testing became a time of revelation. God provided a reprieve from the hot sweltering sun in the shade of the cross mount, and I imagined John the Baptist in our midst. In this hot, dry land, he wore camel's hair clothing with a leather belt around his waist. He said, "After me comes the one more powerful than I, the straps of whose sandals I am not worthy to stoop down and untie" (Mark 1:7-8). He spoke of Jesus and would later baptize Him in the Jordan River. Overwhelmed by God's presence with us, I prayed.

Prayer: *Thank you, Father, for this opportunity to walk where John the Baptist walked and preached. I will not read his sermons the same again. Let them be written on my heart and let them take root in my soul. In Jesus' name, Amen.*

Don't Forget

After a long day on tour, our bus driver stopped at the top of a hill. I heard the familiar words, "Everybody out," and got off the bus with the others. We saw the Temple Mount and a glorious view of Jerusalem. I thought of Jesus' lament: "O Jerusalem, Jerusalem" (Matthew 23:37). The golden dome marked the place where Abraham prepared to sacrifice his son, his only son, Isaac. The two had traveled across the wilderness. Isaac carried the wood and Abraham carried the fire. Centuries later, God's only son, Jesus, would carry the wood—His cross, and He would be the Lamb—the sacrifice. When God saw that Abraham would not hold back anything, even his only son, He provided a lamb in the thicket for the sacrifice.

On this mountain lookout, we shared communion. Eating the bread, which represented Jesus' body, and drinking the wine, the symbol of Jesus' blood of the covenant, I thought I heard Jesus say to me, *Don't forget why I came. Don't forget the miracles and my teaching. Don't forget my sacrifice for your forgiveness and eternal life.* This was a turning point in my journey. I wasn't only walking in the Holy Lands; I was walking closer with God.

Prayer: *Thank you, Father God, for the experience of walking in the Holy Land. At times, we covered more territory than I thought humanly possible, but I am glad I got off the bus every time to be blessed by another reminder of who You are and how much You have done for me. I won't forget! In Jesus' name, Amen.*

Devotions from a Journey Through the Holy Lands

The Way of the Cross

Inside the Church of the Holy Sepulchre, throngs of people waiting to enter the authentic but empty tomb of our Lord Jesus Christ.

The Via Dolorosa means "The Sorrowful Way." It is not mentioned by name in the Bible, but is the path where Jesus carried the cross through Jerusalem to Calvary (Matthew 27:2-27).

It remains a narrow passage today, crowded by store fronts, merchandise and people. I walked to the Church of the Holy Sepulchre, which was once outside town. The church was built over the place where Jesus was crucified, buried and rose from the grave.

I expected to find a hillside very much the same as it was when Jesus suffered and died. Yet, people over the centuries created this beautiful tribute to our Lord. It is a huge and elegant church, and because of the crowds inside, I didn't expect to experience a closeness to God.

Our guide showed us a special marble slab over the place where Jesus was laid. People knelt, cried and prayed. I closed my eyes and asked God to join me there. I lost my inhibitions and knelt. My cheek touched the cold marble. Tears washed over my face, and I whispered, *Thank you, Jesus. Thank you, Jesus.* I thought of how He hung between heaven and hell on the cross to take away my sin. Nothing could have been more personal for me.

Jesus left the glory of heaven to live on earth, to identify with the poor, the sick and sinful people. He was mocked, ridiculed and persecuted. Although He was perfect, He died a criminal's death by a Roman crucifixion. But He was buried as royalty. Joseph of Arimathea, a rich man, had a new tomb carved out of stone for himself, and he laid our Lord Jesus there. He and Nicodemus took Jesus' body down from the cross, carried it to the tomb, wrapped it in cloths and poured myrrh on it. Then they rolled a stone over the entrance (John 19:17).

"On the first day of the week, very early in the morning, the women took the spices they had prepared and went to the tomb. They found the stone rolled away from the tomb, but when they entered, they did not find the body of the Lord Jesus. Suddenly two men in clothes that gleamed like lightning stood beside them. In their fright the women bowed down with their faces to the ground, but the men said to them, 'Why do you look for the living among the dead? He is not here; he has risen! Remember how he told you, while he was still with you in Galilee: 'The Son of Man must be delivered over to the hands of sinners, be crucified and on the third day be raised again'" (Luke 24:1-7).

The most important thing about the tomb, which is also inside the Church of the Holy Sepulchre, is that it is empty. Jesus rose from the grave and will call us home one day:

"In a flash, in the twinkling of an eye, at the last trumpet. For the trumpet will sound, the dead will be raised imperishable, and we shall be changed. For this perishable body must clothe itself with the imperishable, and the mortal body with immortality. Then the saying that is written: 'Death has been swallowed up in victory. Where, O death, is your victory? Where, O death, is your sting?'" (1 Corinthians 15:52-55).

Prayer: *O Lord, you are mighty to save. You took away the sting of death, our sin, and we look forward to living with you forever. In Christ Jesus, Amen.*

A Closer Walk with God

The Good News was Preached

The Garden Tomb, photograph by Brian C. Bush

The Garden Tomb is believed by many to be the place where Jesus was buried. Red, white, pink and violet flowers grow in the garden near the tomb. Trees and shrubs line garden paths. I imagined Mary Magdalene meeting the angel at the tomb. She walked away and suddenly saw Jesus face-to-Face. She heard His voice. Tour groups in the garden sang hymns. This was indeed holy ground.

Archaeologists, however, say this tomb would have been too old at the time of Jesus' burial. This conflicts with the description of the tomb in Luke 23:53: "a tomb cut in stone, where no one had been laid."

A cheerful Jewish guide spoke of our need of a Savior and how that need was met by Jesus. The man's words were sweet to my ears. He preached the good news of Jesus Christ—how He came to teach, heal the sick and raise the dead—how He came to save us from our sins. I saw the image of Christ in this guide's joy, gentleness, peace and simple message. This memory stayed with me weeks after I left Israel. The guide gave away what he could not keep—the love of Jesus. Surely if someone there did not know God's amazing love, he would have experienced it coming through this man. I wondered if the person would have responded by calling on the name of the Lord to be saved (Romans 10:13). He could not do that unless the guide preached the good news.

"How, then, can they call on the one they have not believed? And how can they believe in the one of who they have not heard? And how can they hear without someone preaching to them? And how can they preach unless they are sent? As it is written, 'How beautiful are the feet of those who bring good news!'" (Romans 10:14-15).

Jesus' last will and testament was for His disciples (and all believers) to do as the tour guide did. He said, "All authority in heaven and on earth has been given to me. Therefore, go and make disciples of all nations, baptizing them in the name of the Father and of the Son and of the Holy Spirit, and teaching them to obey everything I have commanded you. And surely I am with you always, to the very end of the age" (Matthew 28:18-20).

These are not only the duties of pastors and church leaders. Through Christ we are a royal priesthood, (1 Peter 2:9) and we are to do what Jesus commissioned.

I know a woman and her son who came to experience God's love through people who fulfilled this command of Jesus. My friend Betty led the two to accept Jesus as their Savior, and my husband Dennis baptized them in a swimming pool. The woman confessed after her baptism, "I feel different." Her joy and peace are etched in my memory. As we follow Jesus, we can make a difference in the lives of others by carrying out God's command to spread the good news of salvation.

Prayer: *Thank you, Lord, for those who are willing and available to speak your truth wherever they are. Empower each of us with gentleness and confidence to follow you and do your will. In Christ Jesus, Amen.*

Trust God First

A view of today's entrance to the City of David

Hezekiah became King of Judah in the City of David in 715 B.C., 255 years after King David's rule. He faced an impossible situation—the onslaught of the Assyrian army. He strengthened his defense in the rolling hills west of Jerusalem, built huge towers to guard gateways of key cities and built supply depots. He made an alliance with Egypt, hoping they would come to his rescue (Isaiah 30:1-2).

Hezekiah blocked the entrance to the Gihon Spring and had a tunnel dug through the hill on which the City of David was built to bring the water within the city walls. He constructed more reservoirs for water and tore down private homes in order to build a massive wall to defend the newer areas of the city (Isaiah 22:10-11).

Hezekiah also paid Sennacherib, the king of Assyria, gold and silver from the house of the Lord to leave the cities of Judah alone (2 Kings 18:14-15).

King Hezekiah depended on his own intelligence and resources, but in all these situations, he did not pray.

Assyrian messengers told the Jews to surrender rather than listen to Hezekiah or trust God. Hezekiah asked Isaiah to pray to his God (2 Kings 19:4) and later, he took the letter from his enemy into the temple and spread it out before the Lord. He finally prayed, and God heard his prayer.

"Therefore this is what the Lord says concerning the king of Assyria: 'He will not enter this city or shoot an arrow here. He will not come before it with shield or build a siege ramp against it. By the way that he came he will return; he will not enter this city,' declares the Lord.

'I will defend this city and save it, for my sake and for the sake of David my servant'" (2 Kings 19:32-34). Although prayer was Hezekiah's last resort, God came to his rescue.

Prayer, however, was Nehemiah's first response when he heard about Jerusalem. A remnant of Israelites lived there inside the crumbled walls, which followed the destruction of 586 B.C. Rather than focus on the impossibility of rebuilding the walls, he prayed:

"Lord, the God of heaven, the great and awesome God, who keeps his covenant of love with those who love him and keep his commandments, let your ear be attentive and your eyes open to hear the prayer your servant is praying before you day and night for your servants, the people of Israel. I confess the sins we Israelites, including myself and my father's family, have committed against you. We have acted very wickedly toward you. We have not obeyed the commands, decrees and laws you gave your servant Moses.

"Remember the instruction you gave your servant Moses, saying, 'If you are unfaithful, I will scatter you among the nations, but if you return to me and obey my commands, then even if your exiled people are at the farthest horizon, I will gather them from there and bring them to the place I have chosen as a dwelling for my Name.'

"They are your servants and your people, whom you redeemed by your great strength and your mighty hand. Lord, let your ear be attentive to the prayer of this your servant and to the prayer of your servants who delight in revering your name. Give your servant success today by granting him favor in the presence of this man" (Nehemiah 1:5-11).

Nehemiah prayed before he asked King Artaxerxes for permission to take leave of his duties as cupbearer to rebuild the walls of his homeland. He prayed when he faced opposition and ridicule from neighboring government officials (Nehemiah 4:4-5). Nehemiah encouraged the people of Jerusalem and they did their part—some in building and some standing guard while the work was being done. In the midst of the construction, Nehemiah heard the outcry of the poor, and he helped them.

Through all this, the wall and its gates were finished in fifty-two days, which seems impossible even with today's modern equipment. Nothing is impossible for God. Will we pray in desperation during tough times as Hezekiah did, or will we pray as Nehemiah did, talking with the Lord each and every day?

Prayer: *O Lord, let us not to be anxious, but to look to you with prayer and thanksgiving. May the peace of God, which passes understanding, guard our hearts and minds in Christ Jesus, Amen.*

The Agony and the Ecstasy

Garden of Gethsemane

The Garden of Gethsemane is at the base of the Mount of Olives. Gethsemane means "pressing of olives." Olive trees have grown there for thousands of years. However, when the Romans destroyed Jerusalem in 70 A.D., they burned down the olive trees. The trees in the garden today are thousands of years old, but they probably grew from the roots of trees that were burned. The olives provide food for nourishment, fuel for light and oil for healing. Like the olives, Jesus is the Bread of life—food for our souls, the Light of the world, and our Great Physician.

Jesus often withdrew to the Mount of Olives to pray. He went there with the disciples after Passover. "My soul is overwhelmed with sorrow to the point of death. Stay here and keep watch with me." Going a little farther, he fell with his face to the ground and prayed, "My Father, if it is possible, may this cup be taken from me. Yet not as I will, but as you will" (Matthew 26:38-39). Later when Jesus came back and found the disciples sleeping, He said, "Watch and pray so that you will not fall into temptation" (Matthew 26:41). He knew what was about to happen and didn't want his friends to sin. Judas led the chief priests and elders to the garden. He betrayed Jesus with a kiss—the beginning of our Lord's suffering.

As olives are crushed to be made useful, our Lord was crushed for our redemption: "He was pierced for our transgressions; he was crushed for our iniquities; upon him was the chastisement that brought us peace, and with his wounds we are healed" (Isaiah 53:5). Death could not hold our Lord! He rose from the grave so we could have eternal life with Him.

Forty days after Jesus' resurrection, He ascended into heaven from the Mount of Olives. "Men of Galilee," they (the angels) said, "why do you stand here looking into the sky? This same Jesus, who has been taken from you into heaven, will come back in the same way you have seen him go into heaven" (Acts 1:11).

According Zechariah 14:4, Jesus will return to the Mount of Olives. "On that day his feet will stand on the Mount of Olives, east of Jerusalem, and the Mount of Olives will be split in two from east to west." Then Jesus will enter the Temple through the East Gate, also called the Gate Beautiful, the gate where Peter healed a crippled beggar.

Our group shared communion in the Garden of Gethsemane. Sirens screamed. Car horns honked. Church bells rang. Men chanted. The noise seemed to violate the reverence of this holy place. Yet, city sounds were there when Jesus prayed, and when He ascended into heaven. The bread and wine, the olive trees and noise—all contributed to the authenticity of the Garden of Gethsemane. This was the place of Jesus' agony.

I walked through the garden among the flowers and ancient olive trees. Tears welled up in my soul as I considered how Jesus prayed for me (John 17), how He suffered and died for me. Then I thought, *the best is yet to come.* Jesus will return some day to the Mount of

Olives, just as He said (John 14:3-4). That will be an ecstasy you and I have never known!

Prayer: *O Lord, it was human of the disciples to fall asleep in the garden from their fatigue. Make us more like Jesus—watchful and ready to meet him when he comes again. In Christ, I pray, Amen.*

A Closer Walk with God

The Healing Pool

Pool of Siloam, photo from Word Generation Bible

Hezekiah's Tunnel begins at the Spring of Gihon and runs through the City of David south to the Pool of Siloam. More than a thousand years after the tunnel was built, Jesus walked in the city. He saw a man who had been blind from birth. The disciples asked Jesus, "Who sinned, this man or his parents, that he was born blind?" (John 9:2). Jesus said, "Neither this man nor his parents sinned, but this happened so that the work of God might be displayed in his life" (John 9:3).

Jesus spit on the ground and made some mud, which he put on the man's eyes. "Go", He said, "and wash in the Pool of Siloam" (John 9:6). The man went to the pool, washed off the mud and went home seeing.

In this very place, more than two thousand years after Jesus healed a man born blind, I walked through the dry part of Hezekiah's Tunnel and stood at the healing Pool of Siloam. I felt a distinct intimacy with God to be in the place where He defended Jerusalem from the Syrians, where Nehemiah repaired the wall going down to the Pool or Siloam (Nehemiah 3:15) and where Jesus healed the man born blind.

All this made me long for a time when I will not only walk in places where the prophets and Jesus walked, but I will see Jesus face-to-Face in the New Jerusalem where there will be no sickness or sadness. God will be our light and life—all we need.

Prayer: *Thank you, Lord Jesus, for the opportunity to walk in the Holy Lands. I look forward to walking with you in the New Jerusalem. In Christ Jesus, Amen.*

Bread of Life

Inside the Church of the Nativity

Bethlehem carries more history and imagery than anyplace in the Holy Lands. In Hebrew, Bethlehem means "house of bread." This gives meaning to Jesus' words, "I am the bread of life," since He was born here (John 6:35). Nearly 30,000 people live in Bethlehem—19% are Christian, which is the largest population of Christians in the Holy Land.

About 4,000 years ago, Jacob buried his wife, Rachel, in Bethlehem. Naomi called it home. Ruth married Boaz in Bethlehem and became the great-grandmother of King David. This was David's home. Samuel anointed David to be king in the midst of his brothers here. However, the event that changed the course of history was the birth of Jesus (Luke 2), fulfillment of Bethlehem prophesy: "But you, Bethlehem Ephratha, though you are small among the clans of Judah,

A Closer Walk with God

out of you will come for me one who will be ruler over Israel, whose origins are from of old, from ancient times" (Micah 5:2).

Angels visited Mary, Joseph and shepherds in the fields. Magi came from the East with gifts for Jesus—gold for a King, frankincense for a Priest, and Myrrh for a Savior. Jesus, our King, Priest and Savior will come again to take those who love Him with all our hearts to be where He is (John 14:2-3).

In 326 A.D. Constantine's mother came to Bethlehem to look for the place where Jesus was born. She paid to have the Church of the Nativity, the oldest church in the world, built over it. The entrance is so low people must bow down to enter. It is so low, animals (horse or camel) cannot go through the door, which makes an easy defense from enemy attack. A fourteen-point silver star marks the exact place of Jesus' birth. It represents 14 generations from Abraham to David and 14 generations from David to Jesus.

Our Jordanian guide taught us that shepherds in Bethlehem raised sacrificial lambs and wrapped them in swaddling cloths. Mary wrapped Jesus, the Lamb of God, in swaddling cloths and laid Him in a manger when He was born. Joseph of Arimathea and Nicodemus took Jesus' body down from the cross of crucifixion, wrapped Him in swaddling cloths, anointed Him with myrrh and laid Him in a tomb. Yet death did not hold Him. He rose from the grave and pushed away the stone so we might live with Him forever. Because He lives, we can face tomorrow with all its triumphs and woes, its joys and sorrows, knowing He is always with us.

Jesus entered this world in Bethlehem of Judah. He lived thirty-three years. His mission was not to turn this world upside down, as many have thought, but to turn it right side up. He wasn't who the Jewish leaders expected as their Messiah, so many of them rejected Him as their Savior. Some believed, however, and preached the good news so we could experience new and everlasting life through Him.

Prayer: *Thank you, Lord, the Bread of Life and the Lamb of God, for saving us from ourselves, for taking away our sin and giving us hope for tomorrow. In Christ Jesus, Amen.*

God Has No Limits

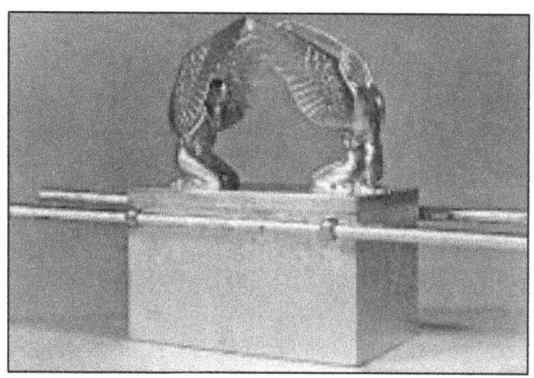

Ark of the Covenant

The name Beth Shemesh means "house of the sun," which means that this Canaanite city was originally dedicated to the sun god. Beth Shemesh is strategically located on the major highway from the Mediterranean coast to Jerusalem. Across the fertile Sorek Valley to the north is the home of Samson, who judged Israel twenty years. This is also the place where the Philistines fought the Israelites before Eli, the priest, died.

Israel lost 4,000 men in the first battle. The elders agreed, then, to take the Ark of the Covenant—the *symbol* of God's presence, into the second battle, thinking it would save them. They were wrong and lost 30,000 men as well as the Ark to the Philistines. God was not limited to the presence of the Ark. He was everywhere, just as He is today. He wanted the Israelites (and us) to talk to Him and trust Him with what seems impossible. Before we judge the Israelites too harshly, let's consider what we put our faith in—our health, wealth, intelligence, power, status, or something else? It would be better for us when we face unbearable circumstances, to talk with God about our concerns and trust Him to help us.

The Philistines took the Ark to the temple of Dagon, the Cannanite god, in Ashdod and put it next to Dagon. The following morning the statue was on its face. The Philistines stood it up, but it fell again. This time its arms and legs came off. The worst consequence was that the people got sick. They called the illness "tumors." Many have believed over the centuries that this is because their lymph nodes swelled into tumor-like proportions. The disease was very contagious and gave the people dysentery. The Philistines carried the Ark from Ashdod, to Gath and Ekron, but people in all five major Philistine cities suffered from the disease. They blamed their suffering on an invasion of rats (1 Samuel 5-6 NIV).

The Philistines finally concluded that their sickness was a result of having the Ark in their cities, and they took it back to the Israelites at Beth Shemesh. They added to it gifts they made of golden tumors and rats.

The sight of the Ark was reason for great celebration among the Hebrew people. However, in their excitement, they ignored the rules that applied to handling the Ark. They looked inside the Ark to see the stone tablets with the Ten Commandments, Aaron's staff that sprouted and the jar of manna, bread from heaven, that fell on Israel in the desert on their way to the Promised Land. As a result of their disobedience, God struck down and killed 70 of their men. It might seem that God was too harsh, but His laws, then and now, are not meant to bring suffering—but to protect and bless His people. We might think that looking inside the Ark would not be harmful, but it robbed the people of their reverence for the holy objects of the tabernacle. These things were not idols, but they represented the holiness and powerfulness of God.

Our God's presence is not limited to holy objects (like the Ark), or a church or a city or country. He promised He would always be present with us and would never leave us. It is better to trust Him, knowing He loves us and cares about what happens to us, than to put our hope in anything or anyone else.

Prayer: *O Lord, help us to know you better and experience your amazing love. Inspire us to look to you when the going gets tough and trust your power to help us—not ourselves or our resources. In Christ Jesus, Amen.*

Five Stones

The Valley of Elah gets its name from the elah tree, a kind of oak or terebinth tree, which grows there. The valley is fertile and green. A battle between the Israelites and the Philistines was fought there. The Israelites trembled in their sandals on one side of the valley and the Philistines camped on the other. Goliath, a giant nearly ten feet tall, stood in the valley and taunted the Israelites. "Why do you come out and line up for battle? Am I not a Philistine, and are you not the servants of Saul? Choose a man and have him come down to me. If he is able to fight and kill me, we will become your subjects" (1 Samuel 17:8-9).

David walked into the valley and faced the giant. He must have looked like a little boy against Goliath. Yet, David said to the giant, "You come against me with sword and spear and javelin, but I come against you in the name of the Lord Almighty, the God of the armies of Israel, whom you have defied. This day the Lord will hand you over to me, and I'll strike you down . . ." (1 Samuel 17:45-46).

David gathered five stones from the Elah Brook. He placed one in his sling and swung it round and round. He released it right at Goliath. The stone penetrated the giant between his eyes and killed him. Then the Israelites chased the Philistines all the way to Ekron and Gath, Goliath's hometown.

We walked down into the dried Elah Brook and picked up stones. I collected five, one for each of my grandchildren. As I gave the stones to the kids, I talked about David and Goliath. "Don't be afraid of anything in this life," I said. "Remember, God is always with you."

Prayer: *O Lord, thank you for always being with us. Thank you that we can trust you and not be afraid. In Christ Jesus, Amen.*

Don't Worry

Lilies of the Field

Do you worry about what you will wear or what you will eat or about the loss of your health or wealth? Jesus addressed our worries in Matthew 6:25-34: "Therefore, I say to you, do not worry about your life, what you will eat or what you will drink; nor about your body, what you will put on. Is not life more than food and the body more than clothing? Look at the birds of the air, for they neither sow nor reap nor gather into barns; yet your heavenly Father feeds them. Are you not of more value than they? Which of you by worrying can add one cubit to his stature?

"So why do you worry about clothing? Consider the lilies of the field, how they grow: they neither toil nor spin; and yet I say to you that even Solomon in all his glory was not arrayed like one of these" (Matthew 6:26 NKJV).

The flowers (not visible) in the picture look like red poppies, and are what Jesus referred to as the lilies of the field. He goes on to say in verse 30: "Now if God so clothes the grass of the field, which is here today and tomorrow is thrown into the oven, will He not much more clothe you, O you of little faith?"

I am glad Jesus used object lessons to teach us how to live. I saw the lilies of the field everywhere when I walked in the Holy Lands, and when I did, I remembered Jesus' words, "Do not worry."

Prayer: *Thank you, Lord Jesus, for vivid pictures that demonstrate your faithfulness. We stand in awe of your deep and unstoppable love. Help us to respond in ways that please you. In your precious name, we pray, Amen.*

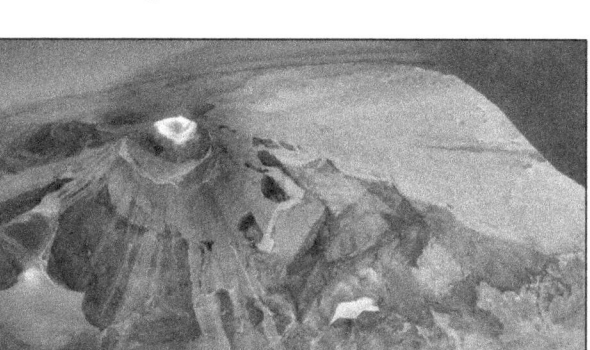

Writing on the Wall

Bell Cave near Mareshah, photo From the Grapevine

Mareshah is in the Shephelah, the low rolling hills of Judah. Its wide fertile valleys are good for agriculture and make travel easy. I learned this is where Herod the Great was born. Although he was king of the Jews, he was not Jewish but an Edomite. The Edomites, descendants of Esau (Genesis 36:8), moved into Judea when the Jews, descendants of Jacob, were taken into Babylonian captivity.

During Herod's reign, Christians were tortured in the amphitheater at Caesarea. Some were beheaded. The ones who survived their torturous wounds fled in an effort to get to the Bell Caves at Mareshah to live their last days. These caves were once quarries and acquired their name by their narrow top and wide circular bottom. The mouths of many of these caves overlooked the plain of Gaza and Ashkelon, Philistine country.

When we visited the largest Bell Cave, 70 feet in diameter and 55 feet high, I saw writing on the wall—crosses and Scripture verses. I touched the carved crosses in the stone. Dying believers wrote words of encouragement for those who would come after them. We sang "Amazing Grace," and the acoustics made our voices sound rich and full, like a concert choir. I was amazed to know people came here to die. Their suffering finally ended in Heaven. No more persecution, torture or pain. Today they are forever in the presence of Jesus our Lord. Hallelujah!

Prayer: *Thank you, Lord, for the hope we have in Heaven. Our bodies will be glorified. There will be no more deformities, disease or pain. As a dear pants for streams of water, so we long for the time we can be with you face to Face. In Christ Jesus, Amen.*

No Complaints

Our bus traveled down the mountain after a visit to the Herodium. All we could see was miles and miles of desert. Then the bus driver pulled to the side of the road, got off the bus and opened the hood. He climbed back inside, made a phone call and talked to our guide. The bus had broken down, but a replacement was on its way. There was no place to hide from the sun beating down on us. The motor was turned off. We had no air conditioning. The doors of the bus were opened. Flies entered. Lots of flies. People used this as a Kodak moment (or Kodak hours). A herd of 400 sheep and a herd of a dozen camels made great pictures. Although the heat seemed debilitating to me, others took photos and videos. No one complained! You might ask why, and I'll tell you. We signed an agreement before we embarked on this journey, that no matter what happened on tour, we would not whine or complain, and we didn't.

John the Baptist, the son of Zechariah, the priest lived in this country. He wore camel hair clothing and a leather belt. Although strange dress for the desert, he preached, "Produce fruit in keeping with repentance . . . The man with two tunics should share with him who has none, and the one who has food should do the same" (Luke 3:8, 11). He said to the tax collectors, "Do not collect more than you are required to" (Luke 3:12) and he said to the soldiers, "Don't extort money and don't accuse people falsely. Be content with your pay" (Luke 3:14).

John rebuked Herod the tetrarch because he married Herodias, his brother's wife. Herod locked him up in prison at the Herodium, high on a mountain in the Judean desert (Luke 3:19-20). We visited the Herodium where Salome, Herodias' daughter danced for King Herod on his birthday. She pleased him so much he promised her anything she wanted, up to half his kingdom. She could have had gold or silver—anything she wanted, even half his kingdom. Shocked by such an offer, Salome ran to her mother. And since Herodias held a grudge against John for his boldness to her and Herod, she prompted Salome to say, "Give me here on a platter the head of John the Baptist" (Matthew 14:8).

Our experience made the stories about John the Baptist in the Bible come alive. We felt the penetrating sun and the scorching heat. I wondered how John could possibly wear camel hair. *How he had the presence of mind to preach?* I didn't complain, but I wanted to. No one complained, but walked in the desert and took pictures. I swatted flies and journaled.

Jesus said of John, "Truly I tell you, among those born of women there has not risen anyone greater than John the Baptist; yet whoever is least in the kingdom of heaven is greater than he" (Matthew 11:11).

John, the forerunner of Christ, prepared the way for Jesus' ministry, yet he was an unsung hero. We can be forerunners too.

God uses our lives for His purpose. As He drew people to John with his weird appearance, he can use things in our lives to show others what He has done. The trials we endure have a fulfillment in the Kingdom of God. Our sin, though forgiven, can be salvaged for God's glory.

Prayer: *Father God, help us not to complain about unpleasant circumstances but to bear fruit in keeping with repentance. Help us to speak the truth boldly as John the Baptist did. Thank you that you are always with us, partnering with us to use our lives for your Glory. In Christ Jesus, Amen.*

Moab Hospitality

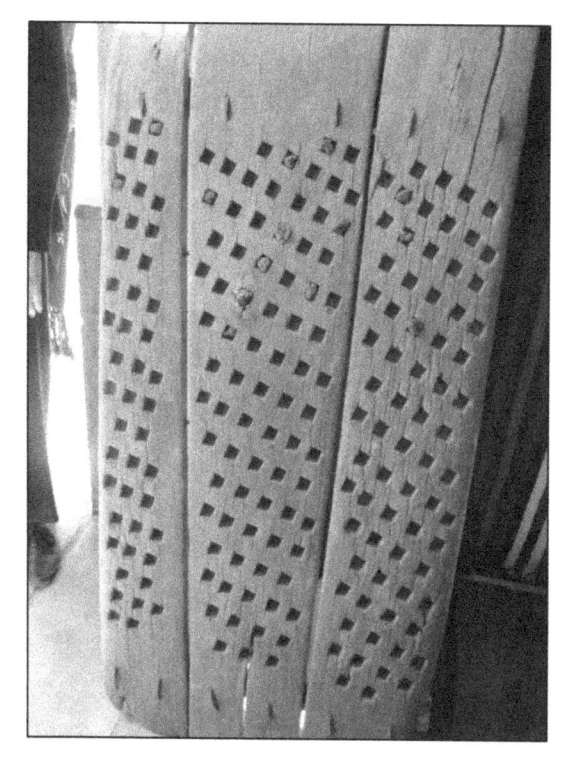

A threshing floor like the one where Ruth met Boaz

We visited Moab, most of which is a high mountain plateau east of the Dead Sea. It is good for growing plants and raising sheep and goats. Mt. Nebo with an elevation of 2,000 feet is in Moab, and is the mountain where Moses viewed the Promised Land. When the Israelites passed through this land on their way to the Promised Land, the Moabites sold them water.

Naomi, Elimelech her husband, and their two sons fled to Moab during a famine in Israel, which was due to Israel walking away from God. Moab accepted the family. The sons married Moabite women, and the families prospered for ten years. Ruth, one of the

Moabite wives, grew to love the ways of the Israelites and their God. When Elimelech and the two sons died, Ruth went with Naomi back to Bethlehem. She said, "Where you go I will go, and where you stay I will stay. Your people will be my people and your God my God." (Ruth 1:18).

The Moabites may not have had the law of God that required good treatment of strangers, but that was what they did. That was part of Ruth's nature. We are called to show kindness to strangers as the Moabites did. God makes it plain in Matthew 25:34-36:

"The King will say to those on his right, 'Come, you who are blessed by my Father; take your inheritance, the kingdom prepared for you since the creation of the world. For I was hungry and you gave me something to eat, I was thirsty and you gave me something to drink, I was a stranger and you invited me in, I needed clothes and you clothed me, I was sick and you looked after me, I was in prison and you came to visit me" (Matthew 25:34-36).

"Do not forget to entertain strangers, for by so doing some people have entertained angels without knowing it" (Hebrews 13:2). Abraham did this even before it was written, when he hurried to provide water to wash three men's feet and then to give them something to eat. He did not know they were angels.

Prayer: *Father God, give us hearts to serve strangers. Help us to be friends to people in need. Open our eyes to opportunities. Open our hearts to show mercy as you show mercy. In Christ Jesus, Amen.*

People of God

Ruins of Jerash, New Testament Gerasa

The earthquake of A.D. 747 devastated Jerash, New Testament Gerasa in what is now Jordan, and left a skeleton of a city in ruins today. Among the many colonnaded streets, temples, churches, theatres and baths, is the graceful Oval Piazza, a stone paved area about 260 feet wide, surrounded by a sidewalk and Ionic columns. So far, eighteen churches have been excavated side by side with pagan temples.

Jerash was founded as a deliberate attempt to change the culture of the residents of Syria and Judea. Founded in Greek language, religion, art, architecture, philosophy and civic administration, it's job was to spread itself by producing similar kinds of communities to produce "citizens of the world." The Jews had a conflict with this practice, because they believed there was only one God, and they were His chosen people. Christians encountered the same problem. Their God would not be identified with any of the pagan deities. They were "people of God," not "citizens of the world," yet they compromised their values by "Christianizing" pagan shrines and beliefs.

A fountain in the atrium of the Cathedral in Jerash flowed with water that turned to wine every year on the anniversary of the miracle Jesus performed at the wedding in Cana (John 2:1-11). The fountain and its surrounding court had been part of an earlier temple to Dionysus, god of wine, an example of Christianizing pagan shrines.

A part of Greek culture, which was incorporated into Christianity, included the use of people's wealth for the public good. Citizens who made donations had their names inscribed on monuments with the amount of their gifts. This is done in American churches today. People who buy pews often have their names engraved on metal plates on the pews they buy. Although this is only one example in existence today, Jesus taught a different standard. He said, "Be careful not to do your acts of righteousness before men, to be seen by them. If you do, you will have no reward from your Father in heaven" (Matthew 6:1).

To what degree can cultural values safely be incorporated into the practice of Christianity, and which ones should be excluded?" The danger of unconsciously accepting our culture into our faith is something we must continue to scrutinize. It takes wisdom, knowing what God desires by reading His word and relying on the counsel of the Holy Spirit. People of God examine cultural influence into their lives against what they know is God's will.

Prayer: *Holy God, teach us how to live our lives pleasing to you in the culture that surrounds us. In Christ Jesus, Amen*

The Lost City

A building carved out of a mountain at Petra

Petra lies east of the Jordan in an area the Bible calls Edom, which means red. It is a city carved out of sandstone mountains, and although the main color is red, it is streaked with purple, pink and white. No building materials or equipment were brought into the canyon, but crafters used hand tools to carve majestic buildings, pillars and sculptures. Carved footholds in the structures were used to advance the work upward instead of using ladders. Some of the buildings appear to be palaces and temples, but were actually tombs. Rows of sandstone seats form a Roman theater to accommodate 3,000 to 4,000 people. Two stone mountains meet on the way into the canyon of Petra. At the bottom is a small opening that challenges horse and rider to go through, often called "the eye of the needle." This gives meaning to the conversation Jesus had with a rich young ruler. He said, "Again I tell you, it is easier for a camel to go through the eye of a needle than for someone who is rich to enter the kingdom of God" (Matthew 19:24, Mark 10:25, Luke 18:25). Even though Edom and Israel have been at odds for thousands of years, their ancestors came from the same family—the Edomites from Esau and the Israelites from Jacob.

The first record of Petra in the Bible happened when Israel defeated five Midianite kings on their way to Canaan. One of the kings, Rekem, is the founder of Petra (Numbers 31:8). The Edomites thought Petra was invincible, but it was conquered by Babylon and Rome. Saul and David also destroyed it. Amaziah, King of Judah, invaded Edom in 801-787 B.C and took the city of Sela, known to us by its Greek name, Petra. When the Babylonians conquered Israel, Edom refused to help her. God had this to say against Edom: "On the day you stood aloof while strangers carried off Israel's wealth and foreigners entered his gates and cast lots for Jerusalem, you were like one of them" (Obadiah 11).

Today Bedouins of Petra serve tourists. The men offer horseback, camel and carriage rides. The young boys sell postcards. The women and young girls sell jewelry. The little children sell multicolored rocks. These families live in caves or tents in Petra or the surrounding area. Young men practiced their English by asking me what I was putting on my skin. I told them it was sunscreen. They wanted some. I squirted a little cream on their arms. They giggled as they rubbed it in and smelled the pleasant scent.

Unlike the Edomites of who failed to meet the needs of Israel, the Bedouins showed us unusual hospitality. You and I have a choice whether we will gloat over someone else's misfortune or offer our help? Jesus said He came to serve instead of being served. Let us follow His example and that of the people who live in Petra today, by cheerfully serving strangers.

Prayer: *Heavenly Father, help us not to consider ourselves better than others but to be willing to serve others, even strangers. In Christ Jesus, Amen.*

The Judgement Seat

The Moses Seat at a Synagogue in Chorazin

The Judgement Seat, also known as The Moses Seat, is found in the ruins of synagogues. The name "Moses Seat" is from Exodus 18:13. After Moses led the Israelites out of Egypt, conflicts rose among the people and they came to Moses. He made judgements from morning until night. His father-in-law, Jethro, saw the daily stress Moses endured and recommended that he delegate leaders to help him by giving solutions to minor disagreements.

In New Testament times this seat was used for teaching the law. Jesus said, "The teachers of the law and the Pharisees sit in Moses' seat. So, you must be careful to do everything they tell you. But do not do what they do, for they do not practice what they preach. They tie up heavy, cumbersome loads and put them on other people's shoulders, but they themselves are not willing to lift a finger to move them" (Matthew 23:3-4). The teachers of the law and the Pharisees corrupted their high calling to sit in the Moses seat.

Leaders today also misuse the power and position given to them to corrupt truth and justice. One day, however, we will all be accountable for the way we lived. Believers will see Jesus seated on the Judgement Seat of Christ. He will recognize how they used the gifts, talents and abilities He gave them and will hand out rewards (crowns). Unbelievers will stand before God at the Great White Throne Judgement (Revelation 20) . They will not receive rewards, but will receive the consequences for rejecting God, His love, forgiveness and a life with Him. This is not what God wanted. He loved the world so much He gave His only Son to be our sacrifice so we would have forgiveness and eternal life. His desire is to give everyone a beautiful inheritance, but we have to accept it. His love, compassion and mercies are new every morning (Lamentations 3:22). He is always with us. We can cast our cares on God, knowing He loves us more than we can imagine. By doing so, we experience peace and fulfillment in life instead of emptiness, anxiety, fear or anger. If you have not experienced God's amazing love and would like to, it is yours for the asking. Pray this prayer: *Father God, I want to experience your love. Please forgive me for the way I have lived and teach me how to live for you. In Jesus' name, Amen.*

If you prayed this prayer, be encouraged. Romans 10:9-10 says, "If you declare with your mouth, "Jesus is Lord," and believe in your heart that God raised him from the dead, you will be saved." Begin now to live your life for Jesus by reading the Bible (start in the book of John) and praying. Sometimes the most powerful prayers are "Thank you, Jesus," or "Help me, Jesus." Then find a Bible-teaching church. May God's face shine on you and be gracious to you.

Prayer: *Heavenly Father, thank you for Jesus, your Son who gave his life for our forgiveness. I pray for any reader who does not know you in a personal way, that they experience your amazing love today. In Jesus' name, Amen.*

A Closer Walk with God

CPSIA information can be obtained
at www.ICGtesting.com
Printed in the USA
BVHW041638081022
648790BV00001B/55